Contents

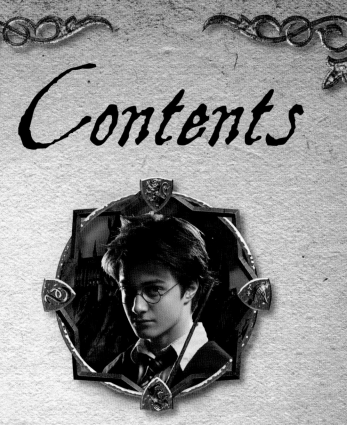

Film Beginnings

Harry Potter always thought he was an ordinary boy. But on his eleventh birthday, Harry finds out a wonderful secret – he's a wizard!

Harry Potter's parents, Lily and James, meet at Hogwarts School of Witchcraft and Wizardry when they are students. They fall in love and eventually get married.

Lily before she starts school at Hogwarts.

James as a Hogwarts student.

When Harry is just a baby, his parents are killed by the evil
Lord Voldemort. He tries to kill Harry, too. Harry survives with
a lightning bolt scar on his forehead as a terrible reminder.

Professors Dumbledore and McGonagall, wizard friends of Harry's parents, bring baby Harry to live with his Muggle relatives, the Dursleys.

Rubeus Hagrid, a wizard and gamekeeper at Hogwarts, brings baby Harry to Privet Drive by flying motorcycle.

Aunt Petunia, Uncle Vernon and Harry's cousin,
Dudley, are horribly mean to Harry.

They never tell Harry the truth about his parents' past.

Harry lives in a cupboard under the stairs.

MR. H. POTTER,
The Cupboard under the Stairs,
4, Privet Drive,
Little Whinging,
SURREY

They don't even give Harry a vitally important piece of post – a letter from Hogwarts School of Witchcraft and Wizardry, inviting him to attend the school.

But Harry's destiny cannot be hindered. The Dursleys are unable to hide the letters from Harry forever.

"*Dear Mr Potter, we are pleased to inform you that you have been accepted at Hogwarts School of Witchcraft and Wizardry...*"

– Letter from Professor McGonagall,
Harry Potter and the Philosopher's Stone film

Harry meets Hagrid again when he comes to take the boy away to his new life at Hogwarts.

Hagrid tells Harry the truth about his parents.

Hagrid takes Harry to Diagon Alley, a place where witches and wizards shop.

Hagrid and Harry go to Gringotts, a wizards' bank run by goblins, to get the money Harry's parents left him.

Then they go to Ollivanders to buy Harry a wand.

"It is curious that you should be destined for this wand when its brother... gave you that scar."

– MR OLLIVANDER, *HARRY POTTER AND THE PHILOSOPHER'S STONE* FILM

To get to Hogwarts, Harry must take the Hogwarts Express from Platform Nine and Three-Quarters at King's Cross station. At the station, Harry meets another boy who is a first year at Hogwarts, Ron Weasley.

"Can you tell me where I might find Platform Nine and Three-Quarters?"

– HARRY POTTER, *HARRY POTTER AND THE PHILOSOPHER'S STONE* FILM

9 ¾

HOGWARTS EXPRESS

Ron's mother tells Harry if he's nervous, he may find it easier to get onto Platform Nine and Three-Quarters if he gets a running start.

Ron and Harry get to know each other
on the ride to Hogwarts.

Ron: "So, so, is it true? I mean, do you really have the . . . the . . . ?"

Harry: "The what?"

Ron: "The scar."

– HARRY POTTER AND THE PHILOSOPHER'S STONE FILM

Later, they are joined by fellow first year, Hermione Granger.

Hermione casts a spell that fixes Harry's broken glasses.

Life at Hogwarts

While at Hogwarts, Harry discovers a world he never knew existed – one filled with wonderful friends and magic!

When students first arrive at Hogwarts, they gather in the Great Hall to be sorted into their houses by the Sorting Hat.

"You must be sorted into your houses. They are Gryffindor, Hufflepuff, Ravenclaw and Slytherin. Now while you are here, your house will be like your family."

– Professor McGonagall, *Harry Potter and the Philosopher's Stone* film

Harry is sorted into Gryffindor, just as both his parents had been.

His new friends are sorted into Gryffindor, too.

Hogwarts is filled with many enchanted
and mysterious objects and creatures.

Fred and George Weasley give
Harry the Marauder's Map.
It shows the location of every
person inside Hogwarts.

Professor
Dumbledore
gives Harry
something
special that
belonged to
his father –
an Invisibility
Cloak.

While exploring an off-limits room at Hogwarts, Harry stumbles upon the Mirror of Erised. In it, he sees the smiling faces of his parents.

"It shows us nothing more or less than the deepest and most desperate desires of our hearts."

— PROFESSOR DUMBLEDORE, *HARRY POTTER AND THE PHILOSOPHER'S STONE* FILM

Classes at Hogwarts are nothing like regular school – they're always exciting, and often challenging.

Harry dreads going to Professor Snape's Potions class. It always seems to Harry as if Snape is out to get him.

Herbology class is taught by Professor Sprout.

Students try to
see the future in
Professor Trelawney's
Divination class.

In flying lessons, Harry discovers his natural talent on a broomstick.

When the students are faced with the threat of Lord Voldemort, Harry secretly teaches his friends how to protect themselves. This group becomes known as Dumbledore's Army.

"*Every great wizard in history has started out as nothing more than what we are now ~ students. If they can do it, why not us?*"

– HARRY POTTER, *HARRY POTTER AND THE ORDER OF THE PHOENIX* FILM

The Triwizard Tournament is a magical contest that takes place between Hogwarts, the Durmstrang Institute and Beauxbatons Academy of Magic. Harry is selected as a contestant for Hogwarts.

The First Task is to retrieve a golden egg guarded by a dragon.

In the Second Task, Harry has to save Ron from the bottom of a black lake, dodging vicious merpeople along the way.

The Third Task is to navigate a treacherous maze to find the Triwizard Cup.

Harry works hard at Hogwarts, but still takes time to have fun and attend special parties.

Harry dances with fellow Gryffindor Parvati Patil at the Yule Ball.

Harry enjoys playing wizard chess with Ron.

Hermione, Harry and Ron visit Hogsmeade on weekends.

There is no pastime Harry enjoys
more than Quidditch.

Professor McGonagall recruits Harry
to be the Seeker for Gryffindor.

Harry
looks up to
Gryffindor's
Quidditch
Captain
and Keeper,
Oliver Wood.

Harry faces his rival Draco Malfoy on the Quidditch pitch.

Quidditch is a tough sport – even tougher when Dementors attack during a match.

Family, Friends and Foes

The friends Harry makes at Hogwarts become his true family – as do his professors and members of the Order of the Phoenix. Hogwarts is also where Harry meets his most powerful enemies.

Harry, Ron and Hermione
form a bond that is truly unbreakable.

"*Maybe you don't have to do this
all by yourself, mate.*"

— RON WEASLEY, *HARRY POTTER AND
THE ORDER OF THE PHOENIX* FILM

"We wouldn't last two days without
her... Don't tell her I said that."

– RON WEASLEY ABOUT HERMIONE GRANGER, *HARRY
POTTER AND THE DEATHLY HALLOWS* – PART 2 FILM

"You need us, Harry."

– HERMIONE GRANGER, *HARRY POTTER
AND THE HALF-BLOOD PRINCE* FILM

Harry's extended family grows during his time at Hogwarts.

In his third year, Harry discovers he has a godfather, Sirius Black.

The Weasleys treat Harry as if he is family.

Harry accompanies the Weasleys to the
Quidditch World Cup.

The Order of the Phoenix, a group of wizards that oppose Lord Voldemort, embraces Harry. Many of the members are Harry's most trusted allies including Professor Dumbledore, Professor McGonagall and Professor Lupin.

Albus Dumbledore

Minerva McGonagall

Kingsley Shacklebolt

Nymphadora Tonks

Remus Lupin

Rubeus Hagrid

Sirius Black

Alastor "Mad-Eye" Moody

Arthur Weasley

Molly Weasley

Neville Longbottom often plays a part in Harry's adventures.

"Things we lose have a way of coming back to us in the end. If not always in the way we expect."

– LUNA LOVEGOOD, *HARRY POTTER AND THE ORDER OF THE PHOENIX* FILM

Harry becomes friends with Ravenclaw student, Luna Lovegood.

Cho Chang, a Ravenclaw, becomes close to Harry when she joins Dumbledore's Army. They even share a kiss in Harry's fifth year.

Harry and Ginny Weasley become more than friends.

Some professors are more interested in
being nasty to Harry than teaching him.

Professor Snape appears to loathe Harry.

*"Clearly fame isn't everything, is it,
Mr Potter?"*

– PROFESSOR SNAPE, *HARRY POTTER
AND THE PHILOSOPHER'S STONE* FILM

Professor Dolores Umbridge, a
Defence Against the Dark Arts
teacher, treats Harry harshly.
She punishes Harry by making
him use a special quill that scars
his hand.

From the moment Harry and Draco Malfoy meet, there is bad blood between them. This hatred extends to Malfoy's parents who are Death Eaters.

"There's not a witch or wizard who went bad who wasn't in Slytherin."

– RON WEASLEY, *HARRY POTTER AND THE PHILOSOPHER'S STONE* FILM

Lord Voldemort was once a student at Hogwarts known as Tom Riddle. Voldemort believes from the Prophecy that Harry is strong enough to defeat him, and therefore wants Harry dead.

"The Prophecy said neither one can live while the other one survives. It means one of us is going to have to kill the other in the end."

– HARRY POTTER, *HARRY POTTER AND THE ORDER OF THE PHOENIX* FILM

Beasts
and
Creatures

Over the eight Harry Potter
films, Harry meets all sorts
of amazing magical creatures
and strange beasts.

A few magical creatures become
Harry's trusted friends and allies.

Harry's snowy owl, Hedwig, is a gift from Hagrid.

Dobby the house-elf befriends Harry and tries his best to help him on a number of occasions.

"Dobby has come to rescue Harry Potter, of course."

– DOBBY, *HARRY POTTER AND THE DEATHLY HALLOWS – PART 1* FILM

Harry tricks Lucius Malfoy into releasing Dobby from slavery.

Harry also meets magical creatures that belong to his professors at Hogwarts.

Fawkes, Professor Dumbledore's Phoenix, comes to Harry's aid while he's in the Chamber of Secrets.

"Of course, Phoenix tears have healing powers."

– HARRY POTTER, *HARRY POTTER AND THE CHAMBER OF SECRETS* FILM

Hagrid and Harry with Aragog, Hagrid's beloved pet spider.

Harry with Buckbeak, Hagrid's Hippogriff.

Some creatures that Harry encounters
come in handy for making a daring exit.
Harry, Ron and Hermione escape
Gringotts on the back of a dragon.

"*Brilliant. Absolutely brilliant.*"

– Ron Weasley, *Harry Potter and the Deathly Hallows – Part 2* film

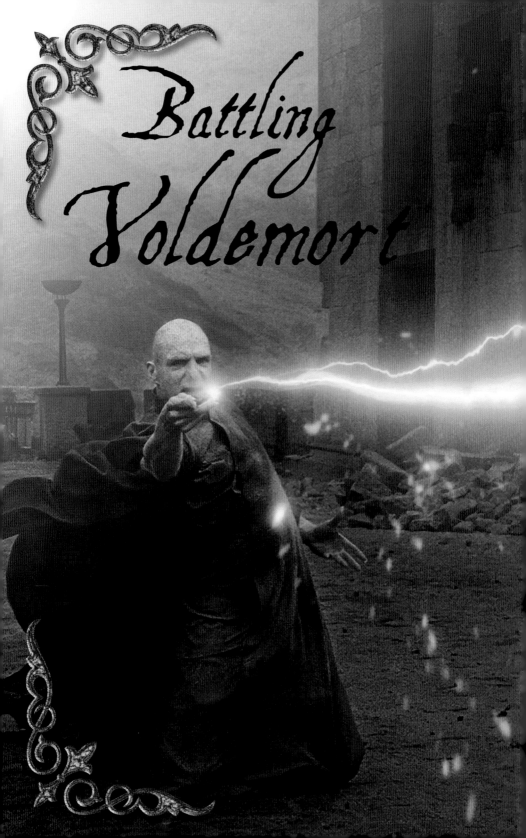

Battling Voldemort

During his time at Hogwarts, Harry has several near-deadly battles with Lord Voldemort. For most encounters, Harry has his friends by his side; however in their last explosive battle, Harry fights the Dark Lord on his own.

During the Third Task of the Triwizard Tournament, Harry and Voldemort come face to face in their first duel. Harry barely escapes with his life.

In Harry's fifth year, Dumbledore intervenes just as Voldemort is about to kill Harry. They have an explosive duel in the Ministry of Magic.

Harry and Voldemort's final battle
takes place at Hogwarts.

"Come on, Tom. Let's finish this the
way we started it – together."

– Harry Potter to Voldemort, Harry Potter
and the Deathly Hallows – Part 2 Film

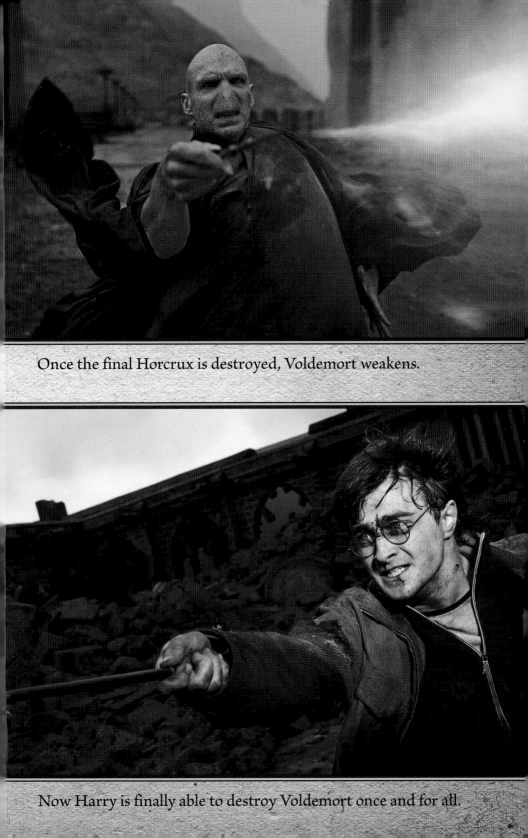

Once the final Horcrux is destroyed, Voldemort weakens.

Now Harry is finally able to destroy Voldemort once and for all.

"Working hard is important, but there's something that matters even more. Believing in yourself."